Animals Close Up

BIRDS CLOSE UP

By Seth Lynch

Gareth Stevens Publishing

Please visit our website, www.garethstevens.com. For a free color catalog of all our high-quality books, call toll free 1-800-542-2595 or fax 1-877-542-2596.

Library of Congress Cataloging-in-Publication Data
Names: Lynch, Seth, author.
Title: Birds close up / Seth Lynch.
Description: New York : Gareth Stevens Publishing, [2023] | Series: Animals close up | Includes index.
Identifiers: LCCN 2021040566 (print) | LCCN 2021040567 (ebook) | ISBN 9781538281161 (set) | ISBN 9781538281178 (library binding) | ISBN 9781538281154 (paperback) | ISBN 9781538281185 (ebook)
Subjects: LCSH: Birds–Juvenile literature.
Classification: LCC QL676.2 .L96 2023 (print) | LCC QL676.2 (ebook) | DDC 598–dc23
LC record available at https://lccn.loc.gov/2021040566
LC ebook record available at https://lccn.loc.gov/2021040567

First Edition

Published in 2023 by
Gareth Stevens Publishing
29 East 21st Street
New York, NY 10010

Editor: Kristen Nelson
Designer: Rachel Rising

Photo credits: Cover, p.1 Lorcel/Shutterstock.com; p.5 Agustin J. Villarreal/Shuttestock.com; pp. 7, 24 Maciej Olszewski/Shutterstock.com; p.9 Ksenia Shestakova/Shutterstock.com; p. 11 Alan Tunnicliffe/Shutterstock.com; pp. 13, 24 Panu Ruangjan/Shutterstock.com; p. 15 John C Evans/Shutterstock.com; pp. 17, 24 Polishchuk Elena/Shutterstock.com; p. 19 David Herraez Calzada/Shutterstock.com; p. 21 Nagel Photography/Shutterstock.com; p. 23 Cuson/Shutterstock.com.

Printed in the United States of America

CPSIA compliance information: Batch #CSGS23: For further information contact Gareth Stevens, New York, New York at 1-800-542-2595.

Contents

Birds live all over the world.
There are thousands of kinds.

Birds have a beak.
It is hard.
It is used to eat.

Birds have two eyes.

Owls have large eyes.
This helps them see
in the dark.

Birds are covered
in feathers.
Feathers keep birds dry
and warm.

They help birds blend in.

Birds have two wings. Most birds use wings to fly.

Penguins don't use their wings to fly. They swim!

All birds have two feet. Most birds have three or four toes.

Ostriches only have two toes!

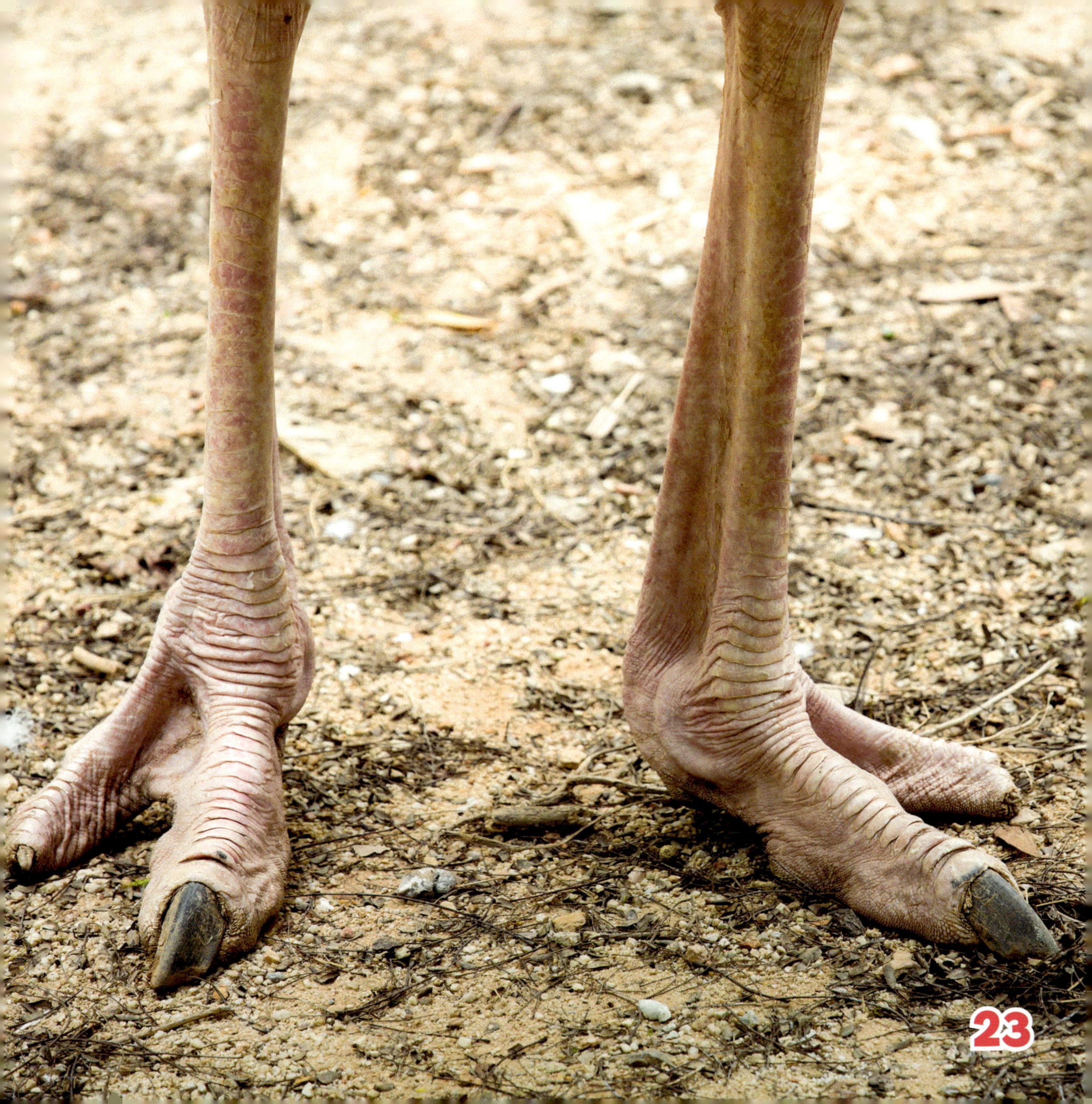

Words to Know

beak

feathers

wings

Index